Punctuation Repair Kit

Why bother?

Punctuation matters.
For exams, life, everything.
You need to say what you mean.
You should mean what you say.
You don't want to look stupid!

Text copyright © 1996 William Vandyck
Illustrations copyright © 1996 David Farris

Designed by Claire S. Pritchard

Cover illustration by Mark Oliver

First published by Hodder Children's Books in 1996
This edition first published in 2005

A Catalogue record for this book is available from the
British Library.

ISBN 0 340 89334 6

Hodder Children's Books
A division of Hodder Headline Limited
338 Euston Road
London NW1 3BH

Printed and bound in Great Britain by Bookmarque Ltd, Croydon, Surrey

Punctuation Repair Kit

Improve Your Punctuation Skills

WILLIAM VANDYCK

Hodder Children's Books

a division of Hodder Headline Limited

This book is dedicated to my friend,
Snidey Kathy.

W.V.

CONTENTS

7	Introduction
11	Sentences and paragraphs
22	Capital letters
27	Full stops
30	Question marks and exclamation marks
35	Commas
51	Brackets
54	Colons
60	Semi-colons
66	Dashes and dots
74	Apostrophes
87	Quotation marks
95	The final test
96	MOP certificate

INTRODUCTION

The Big Question: Why Bother?

Punctuation matters. Just accept it.
A lot of people say...

> But what about all those really difficult hurdles in life?

> Like schoolwork?

> Exams?

> Getting interviews for jobs?

> Getting on in your job?

> Hmm? What are they all saying?

Well, put it this way: you can go a long way in all things in life if you observe

GOLDEN RULE NUMBER ONE

It is simple.
It is easy to remember.
It is **absolutely crucial.**
And it is over the page.

DON'T LOOK STUPID!

There are right ways to punctuate, and there are wrong ways.

If you use the wrong way, it might not be clear what you're saying. Or, worse, you may be saying something you don't mean. What will people think?

Now, this book is going to help. And you won't be alone in your learning.

We're going to go to the Repair Kit Garage. I'd like you to meet the mechanics.

Here's Zelda. Say hello, Zelda.

Hello. Welcome to the garage.

Here's Steven, the Stupid Monster. Say hello, Steven.

Goodbye... Oh – what was the question again?

Oh dear. Here's Colin.

Hello, I want to be a teacher. I may sound dull, but I do collect gravel. I know that sounds a bit dull too. It is, I suppose. In fact, it's pretty much a waste of time. Sorry!

Er, thank you, Colin. Well, you have a quick practice at being a teacher. Steven can make some tea, and we'll make a start.

OK, everybody. I may be dull, but I can summarise things in a clear and neat way.

COLIN'S CONCLUSIONS PAGE

Punctuation matters.
For exams, life, everything.
You need to say what you mean.
You should mean what you say.
You don't want to look stupid!

SENTENCES AND PARAGRAPHS

POW!

First, we'll look at possibly the hardest thing to lay down fixed rules about in the whole of the English language! How about that? We are clearly not messing about here. Oh no, we are cracking on with the difficult issues straight away.

THE Why Baby

Whhyyy start with something hard?

It's like understanding about car engines. A car engine is easy to recognise, but it's a bit difficult to say exactly what a car engine *is* because there are so many different types. Once you understand what a car engine is, you'll find it easier to understand the individual bits inside it.

It's the same with sentences and paragraphs. Like car engines, they are easy to spot, and hard to define. But it will help you to understand and use bits of punctuation if you first get a general idea of what sentences and paragraphs are all about.

So, here's what you need to know about sentences and paragraphs.

SENTENCES
The Easy Bit

First, a rule which is very easy and tremendously important.

Every sentence starts with a capital letter and finishes with a full stop.
Like that one – and this one.

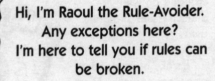

Hi, I'm Raoul the Rule-Avoider.
Any exceptions here?
I'm here to tell you if rules can
be broken.

There are no exceptions, OK?
None! Not even question
marks (?) and exclamation
marks (!) like the ones I've just
used. We'll be dealing with those later, but
for the moment, just remember that they have built-
in full stops at the bottom. So they do end sentences by making sure
the full stop is there! Understand?

It is a fantastically easy rule to remember. Because it is
fantastically easy, if you get it wrong, you will absolutely, definitely,
no-doubt-about-it, look

STUPID.

Enjoy this moment. Savour it for all you can. This rule about sentences is one of the few things in punctuation that has no exceptions. Take any page of this book. Or any book. You should find that every single sentence begins with a capital letter and ends with a full stop. This is so straightforward that even Steven should be able to get it right.

Oh, and thanks for the tea, Steven.

i sentence myself to death for forgetting to put a capital letter at the beginning of this sentence.

This is known as capital punishment.

OK. We've dealt with the bits at the ends of sentences. But what goes in the middle? This is not so easy.

Probably the best way to think about a sentence is to remember two things:

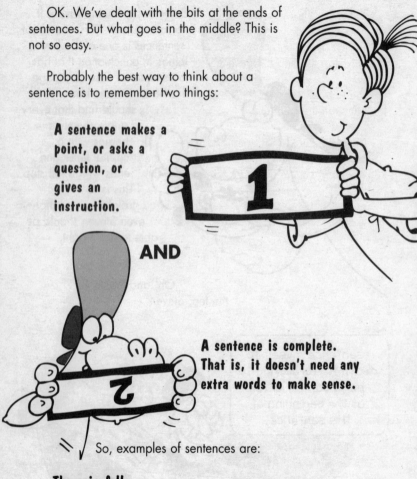

A sentence makes a point, or asks a question, or gives an instruction.

AND

A sentence is complete. That is, it doesn't need any extra words to make sense.

So, examples of sentences are:

The rain fell.
That sentence about the rain was really boring.
The man's head came clean off.
That's better, isn't it?
Don't answer back.

Have a quick check that those sentences stick to our two rules.

Remember that you can't tell a sentence by how long it is.

In fact, by making one of our example sentences longer, we can actually stop it being a sentence. For example:

The rain fell. ◄——————— **This is a sentence.**
Although the rain fell. ◄——————— **This is not a sentence.**

The last example isn't really complete, is it? The word "Although" suggests that something happened **despite** the rain. Yet we don't know what it is. We're left hanging in the air.

But we can make it back into a sentence again by completing the sense. For example, by saying:

Although the rain fell, the game continued.

Now there is a complete point. That's what we can call a sentence.

Try these examples. Which of them do you think are sentences?

Question 1
a) Spinning wildly through the air, humming quietly.
b) She bit him.

Answer 1

✗ a) No. Obviously there's lots going on (and it all sounds very exciting). But it's not complete in sense, is it? We need some extra words for the sense to be complete.

✓ b) Yes! It may be short but it makes a point and it is complete. You don't need extra words for it to make sense on its own. It sounds quite fun.

Now have a go at making sentences from the following passage.

Question 2

there was a terrible collision on the motorway a lorryload of jelly wobbled so much that it fell into the road this caused a lorry carrying custard to slide into a van delivering sponge cake local residents sprinkled hundreds and thousands onto the resulting mixture to stop it being so slippery the police said that traffic would be a trifle delayed

In case you thought punctuation was pointless, look how much easier this is to read when it's properly punctuated.

Answer 2

There was a terrible collision on the motorway. A lorryload of jelly wobbled so much that it fell into the road. This caused a lorry carrying custard to slide into a van delivering sponge cake. Local residents sprinkled hundreds and thousands onto the resulting mixture to stop it being so slippery. The police said that traffic would be a trifle delayed.

Advanced Students Only

Hold onto your hats because here's where we enter "Sometimes it's OK to break the rules" territory. Look at this passage.

Ah ha**!** About time we had an exception**!**

Zelda threw herself out of the way of the car. A squeal of brakes. The crunch of metal. Glass smashing. Flames. An explosion. And then, more frightening still, silence.

Obviously the writer of this piece of action fiction hasn't used full sentences, but the short sentences are used to speed up the pace of the writing. It would have been a bit dull if it had read:

There was a squeal of brakes. Then there was a sound of metal crunching. Then there was the sound of glass smashing...

Style is one of the main reasons it's sometimes difficult to say exactly what a sentence is and isn't. But don't let that get you down. If you remember the general rules, you'll have a much better idea of when you can break them, and when other people who are breaking them are being stylish... or

Problems

Often people use full stops where there doesn't appear to be a full sentence. Sometimes they are being stupid, eg. Although it was raining. But sometimes it's OK just to use a bit of a sentence.

GREETINGS

You'll probably find it easier to think of these as exceptions. In fact, often they're short versions of sentences which were so frequently used that people didn't bother getting to the end of them. ("Morning" is short for "Good morning", which is short for "I wish you a good morning", and "Yo!" is short for "You". Someone must have been in a real hurry).

QUESTIONS AND ORDERS

We've already said that a sentence can give instructions and ask questions, but we also said that a sentence should be complete in itself. You might think that "Don't!" and "Why not?" aren't complete. But because these words are usually only said in response to something happening, or in answer to something someone says, they usually do make sense on their own. For instance, if you were about to strike a match and someone said "Don't!", to which you replied, "Why not?" these words would make sense. They would be short for:

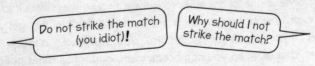

ANSWERS

"A bucketful of spanners" is not a sentence because it doesn't make sense on its own. But if it were the answer to a question it would make sense, be complete and be followed by a full stop. So answers which aren't really sentences can end in full stops.

PARAGRAPHS
The Easy Bit

A paragraph contains a sentence or a number of sentences. It always starts on a new line. It is usually indented (which means the first line begins slightly in from the left-hand side of the page.)

The Useful Bit

How long should sentences and paragraphs be? When do you need to start a new sentence or a whole new paragraph?

The best general rule is:

Think of your reader. Think what would make things easier to read and understand.

Really, it's a matter of style and judgment. A good general tip is to keep your writing lively by having sentences of different lengths.

Someone once said that a paragraph is "A unit of thought, not of length… " This is a pretty good way of thinking about it. A paragraph ends where you've come to a break in a thought, or a topic, or a section of description. In this break the reader and the writer can draw breath. The next thing will be something new – which is why it is started on a new line.

Next time you write, try it out!

The bad news is that you can't just start a new paragraph every time you start a new sentence. And you can't ignore paragraphs either. See if you can find a page in a book with no paragraphs. Doesn't it look terrible? Is that how you want your writing to look?

The good news is that as long as you stick to the general rules, you'll do just fine.

Let's try another way of looking at it. What's the one thing on a car that you really must have?

Thank you, Zelda. You need brakes because you can't just go on and on. Sometimes you just have to stop. It's the same when you're writing – it's important to make sure the breaks work. This is why you use sentences and paragraphs.

Three helpful hints

1 Short sentences are easier to understand, but don't use only short ones. You can. If you want to. But it's jerky. It's a bit irritating. Isn't it?

2 Long sentences are sometimes more elegant than a series of short ones but if you make them too long, or have too many long ones, your reader may get a bit lost, or bored; I mean by the time a sentence has been going on as long as this one, you've really got to wonder whether it wouldn't be better to have several sentences instead, haven't you? Hello? Is there anyone still reading this bit?

3 You will get a better feel for paragraphing if you take a look at what other people do. Next time you're reading something, keep an eye on when the writer has started a new paragraph, and ask yourself, "Why?".

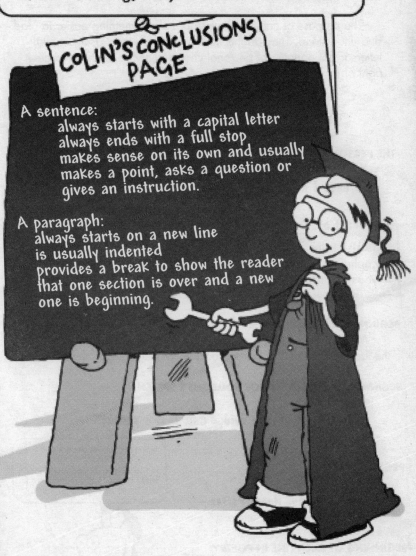

I do want to make this absolutely clear—I know it's a bit boring, but you have to be sensible.

COLIN'S CONCLUSIONS PAGE

A sentence:
always starts with a capital letter
always ends with a full stop
makes sense on its own and usually makes a point, asks a question or gives an instruction.

A paragraph:
always starts on a new line
is usually indented
provides a break to show the reader that one section is over and a new one is beginning.

CAPITAL LETTERS

The purpose of capital letters is to make something easier to read and understand. They do this in a number of ways. Using capital letters is not a matter of personal choice or style. You have to get it right or look **STUPID.**

When to use a capital letter

THE PERSONAL PRONOUN "I"

You use a capital letter when you say "I" for example,

I hope I never have to repeat this.

Fact box

Turkish is the only language in the whole world in which the capital "I" is dotted. So, don't dot your capital "I", unless you're writing Turkish.

BEGINNING EVERY SENTENCE

We have already looked at this. If you've forgotten, slap yourself in the face with a wet fish, then go back to the beginning of the book.

BEGINNING A QUOTATION OF SOMEONE'S SPEECH

For example:

The man sat up and said, "Call that a punch?"

PEOPLE'S NAMES

Names are easy:

James, Kathy, Harry Potter —
these all have capital letters.

Some people say I'm a dimwit,
Some people say I'm thick,
But all of them have to admit,
That I can write poems that rhyme,
well, apart from this one.

BEGINNING OF EACH LINE IN POETRY

PROPER NOUNS

Well, this is tricky, but understanding the difference between a proper noun and other words helps to avoid the most common mistakes with capital letters.

First you should know that when a word names – "identifies" – a thing, we call it a noun. So, nouns include: dog, pavement, time, panic. (From the last two examples, you'll see that it's not always objects – it can be things you can't hold or look at).

Now, when a noun is being used as a name, or part of a name for a specific person or thing, it is called a "proper noun" and gets a capital letter.

Zelda, could you give us an example?

Jargon Alert! Jargon Alert! What is a proper noun?

JARGON MONSTER

The only prince I have met is Prince Charles, whose dog I fed.

The straightforward naming word is "prince". There are many princes but there is one particular prince that Zelda is talking about here – Prince Charles.

So, the very same word (prince) gets used with and without a capital letter – what matters is not the word itself but **how** the word is being used.

ROYAL DOGGY CHOCS

The following are sometimes listed as the types of names which need capital letters

- Books, songs, plays, etc.: "Charlie and the Chocolate Factory"

- People: Mrs Evans, Sir Lancelot, Lady Penelope, Little Lord Fauntleroy

- Organisations, events, etc.: The Post Office (but "the post office at the corner")

- Countries, towns, rivers, etc.: Patagonia, London, Finsbury Park, the Mississippi River

- Planets: Saturn, Pluto

- Nicknames: "Dopey" Kent, "Kippers" Hancock

- Deity: God, Buddha, Allah. Carry this on if you're talking about Him, His, He, etc.: God spoke, and He was angry.

- Days, months, etc.: Monday, January, Christmas Day

- Rulers/titles: Duke of York, The Queen of England (but "a meal fit for a queen")

- Geographical areas: The West (as opposed to the direction – to the west)

- Brand names: You can clean your room with a hoover or a Hoover, really. Strictly speaking it should have a capital letter, but the word has become so commonly used for "vacuum cleaner" that it is OK to use it without one. The same goes for "biro" but not Police sunglasses. Having police sunglasses would probably get you into trouble, anyway.

Are there any other times when we should use capital letters?

Please, no more!

Try putting in the capital letters.

Question 1

the goalkeeper, peter bonnetti, was known as "the cat" because he was as agile as a cat.

[start of sentence]

[We are just talking about one goalkeeper, but it's just a noun – not a proper noun – as the word goalkeeper isn't being used as part of the name of the goalkeeper.]

Answer 1

The goalkeeper, Peter Bonetti, [name] was known as "The Cat" [name] because he was as agile as a cat.

[No capital letter as it is just a noun, not part of a name.]

Question 2

although he always wanted to travel north to the north pole, there were few banks in the west who would pay him these days. still he said he had to start by the first of january so i wished him the best of luck and told him not to worry that his nickname was "the absolute loser".

[name]

[start of sentence]

[name of area, rather than direction]

Answer 2

Although he always wanted to travel north to the North Pole, there were few banks in the West who would pay him these days. Still he said he had to start by the first of January, so I wished him the best of luck and told him not to worry that his nickname was, "The Absolute Loser".

[easy]

[nickname]

[name of month]

25

FULL STOPS

There are two uses for full stops. One is to show the end of a sentence, as we have already seen. The other is for abbreviations.

Jargon Alert! Jargon Alert! What are abbreviations?

Abbreviations are just shortened versions of words, and sometimes you use a full stop in them. For example, "U.S.A." is an abbreviation of "United States of America".

There are two rules that you should know about abbreviations.

When you're putting initials in place of first names, you always put a full stop after each initial. For example, William George Vandyck can be written W.G.Vandyck.

The second rule is that when a word is contracted so that you're left with an abbreviation made up of the first and last letters of the word, you don't have to put a full stop. So:

Mr (Mister) Thompson killed Dr (Doctor) Evans on Mt (Mount) Everest with Lt (Lieutenant) Smith's hockey stick.

OK, now you know what it's all about, put your hand over the right-hand side of the next page and see if you know abbreviations for those on the left-hand side.

December	Dec.
Mister	Mr
Her Majesty's Ship Dreadnought	H.M.S. Dreadnought
Automobile Association	A.A.
Royal Automobile Club	R.A.C.
British Broadcasting Corporation	B.B.C. or BBC
European Union	E.U. or EU
leg before wicket	l.b.w. or lbw
eight o'clock in the morning	8:00 a.m. or 8.00 am
For example	e.g. or eg

Hold on, hold on!
What on earth is going on here?
B.B.C. or BBC?
Don't you know the answers?

Yes, I know, I'm sorry, but the fact is that apart from the two rules I mentioned, it's a bit vague. There isn't much of a general rule. What keeps happening is that a perfectly reasonable abbreviation gets made up, like "B.B.C.", then it gets used so often that the full stops get dropped. Nowadays people tend to write BBC, rather than B.B.C. On the others, the full stops are being dropped more and more, but you still can't really say that putting them in is wrong.

If you're in doubt, put them in.

QUESTION MARKS AND EXCLAMATION MARKS

Question Marks

A Question Mark Looks Like This: ?

The rule is quite simple. If someone is asking a direct question, put a question mark at the end of it.

> What do you call a man with a plank on his head?
> ˙pɹɐʍpƎ

Now, although the rule has no exceptions, there is one thing that sometimes causes confusion.

DIRECT AND INDIRECT QUESTIONS

It is important to tell the difference between "direct" questions and "indirect" questions.

Jargon Alert!
Jargon Alert!
What are these direct and indirect questions?

It's best explained by examples.

Look at this conversation:

"Can you keep quiet?" I asked him.
"Do you want a punch in the mouth?" he replied.

Now, these are called **direct** questions. The direct question is the question exactly as it was spoken – with a question mark at the end of it.

Instead, of course, you could decide to write about the same conversation like this:

I asked him if he could keep quiet. He asked me
whether I wanted a punch in the mouth.

These are called **indirect** questions. "Indirect" means that we don't actually hear the question itself but instead we are told indirectly what the question was.

Any question in the whole world can be set out directly or indirectly, and you only put a question mark if it's direct.

Okay, your turn. Where should you have question marks in this lot?

Terry was thinking about what he should do.
"Do you want to go out" June asked, hopefully.
"With you" he asked. She looked me at him angrily and wondered if he thought she could mean anyone else. "Do you really think I want to go out with you" he laughed, heading for the balcony. She picked up the huge teddy bear with "Will you marry me" on its T shirt - was it really only two weeks ago that he had given it to her - and flung it at him.

Here are the answers. [Yes! Direct question]

[No question mark - indirect question.]

Terry was thinking about what he should do. "Do you want to go out?" June asked, hopefully. [No. Indirect question.]

[Yes! Direct question] "With you?" he asked. She looked at him angrily and wondered if he thought she could mean anyone else. "Do you really think I want to go out with you?" he laughed, heading for the balcony. She picked up the huge teddy bear with "Will you marry me?" on its T shirt - was it really only two weeks ago that he had given it to her? - and flung it at him.

[Yes! Direct question]

[Yes! Direct question - it's the T shirt that's asking the question!]

[Yes - a sneaky direct question in her thoughts]

Have you finished? Let's move on to the exclamation mark...

[Yes! Direct question]

Exclamation Marks

An Exclamation Mark Looks Like This: !

You shouldn't use it too often and there are three things to remember about it.

You can use it for emphasis. You can use it to show humour. You can use it for irony.

First let's look at **emphasis.**

From the name "exclamation mark" you can tell that it means that something is being "exclaimed". So shout it out! Give it more emphasis – like this!

Now how about **humour?**

Sometimes people add an exclamation mark to a sentence to make it clear that they mean it to be funny. It's like adding a wink at the end. For example:

Jason fell over – it served him right!

For this term's play, we would be grateful if parents could send in any old sheets – washed whiter than white first, please!

If there were no exclamation marks after these, they would still make perfect sense, but they would seem to be much more serious wouldn't they?

Irony is less obvious, but don't panic! You'll probably get the hang of it quite quickly. This is a bit like the "humour" point. Sometimes people get across what they mean by saying the opposite in a particular tone of voice. This is called "irony", or, if it's insulting, "sarcasm".

Jargon Alert! Jargon Alert! What is this irony?

For example, imagine Zelda lent Steven her tools and that he broke them, and didn't offer to replace them. Zelda might say:

> I think that this is not very friendly. I feel unable to rely on you further. You get no thanks from me for this behaviour.

But come on, get real! No one talks like this. She's much more likely to say the following, in a slightly sarcastic tone of voice which makes it clear that she means the opposite:

> Well, you're a really good friend. I really feel I can rely on you. Thanks a lot.

Now we have a small problem. If you just write the words out, they obviously mean the opposite of what Zelda says. So, what we do is add an exclamation mark to show that Zelda's words are meant to be ironic:

> Well, you're a really good friend! I really feel I can rely on you. Thanks a lot!

Don't Overuse It!

It's as simple as that! It's easy to see why you shouldn't! It becomes extremely hard to read! Really trying! Remember – some people don't like to read them at all! Let alone several on the same page! So before you use two or more together like this !!, or this !!!, just remember this: Don't look

STUPID.

COMMAS

A Comma Looks Like This: ,

It is tremendously useful because it does all sorts of jobs. Often people use it in the wrong way which makes them look **stupid** in all sorts of ways. So settle down, because this one is going to take the longest to go through.

Different Pauses

As you know, a full stop brings a sentence to an end. Well, basically, a comma means a slight pause in a sentence.

We'll come to the many uses of these pauses in a moment, but first, this:

All commas are pauses, but not all pauses are commas.

Sometimes the pause is dealt with best by finishing the sentence, and starting a new one.

Sometimes you show a pause in a sentence in a different way; by a semi-colon perhaps – or a dash (or brackets) – or a colon:

Sometimes where you would pause if you were reading aloud, you don't need to put anything. For example, imagine you are telling someone this news-story joke:

> Every half an hour, a person is knocked down in a road traffic accident. He's sick and tired of it.

When telling this you might very well pause slightly after "every half an hour". But the words "Every half an hour a person is knocked down… " make sense (and in the way you want them to) without a pause, so you don't need the comma.

OK. Now let's have a look at the different uses of the comma.

But I've got the general idea that a comma means a slight pause in a sentence — whhyyy do I need to know any more than that?

As you'll see, you can make yourself look very **stupid** if you don't use commas correctly. Whether you should use one, and where you should put it if you do, depends on what you are trying to say. This is why we need to consider all these various uses separately. Just for now, Why Baby, bear in mind this true story about someone who didn't use a comma correctly.

In the U.S.A. the government wanted to allow fruit-plants to be duty free. So no-one would have to pay a tax if they wanted to bring them into the country. But instead of writing:

All foreign fruit-plants are free from duty.

a clerk wrote:

All foreign fruit, plants are free from duty.

That meant that there were two things that were duty free: all fruit and all plants. So the government wouldn't get tax on all sorts of things – not just fruit-plants.

A tiny slip cost the government millions of dollars and made them look

STUPID.

Uses of a Comma

We've seen that commas are usually used as a way of separating the words within a sentence to make it easier to understand. Here is a list of ways commas can do this. We'll come back and consider each of them separately:

To set apart extra points
Colin was, despite his dull stories, the most exciting tiddlywink player of his generation.

To separate items in a list
Please place all watches, rings, jewellery, silly hats, money and valuables in the hotel safe.

To set apart the people being addressed from the rest of the sentence
It seemed like a good idea at the time, officer.

To introduce direct speech
The man ran across the beach shouting, "Jellyfish! Jellyfish!"

To introduce questions
You are going to give me this video back, aren't you?

To emphasise something
I started fighting because I felt like it, that's why.

To balance two things that are being compared
The taller they are, the farther they have to reach for their shoelaces.

Right, let's go through them.

**Colin was, despite his dull stories, the most
exciting noughts and crosses player of his generation.**

You can use commas to show which words are the main part of a
sentence and which are less important, extra points.

In our example, the main point is that Colin was the most exciting
noughts and crosses player. There is an extra point, which is that this
was even though he told really boring stories. We put the commas
around the extra point to make it clear for the reader.

When we use them like this, commas are like brackets (which we
haven't looked at yet, but which look like this). But there is a
difference between commas and brackets. You always have to use
two brackets, but you can use just one comma together with the
break that you get with the start and finish of the sentence. For
example, the news about Colin could be written like this:

**Despite his dull stories, Colin was the most exciting
noughts and crosses player of his generation.**

or

**Colin was the most exciting noughts and crosses
player of his generation, despite his dull stories.**

In all three examples the words "despite his dull stories" are
clearly packaged off. In our first example, they're packaged off
between the two commas. In the last, it's between the comma and
the end of the sentence.

If I can do this with brackets, whhyyy do I need to think about it with commas?

A fair question. Here are the reasons.

Style

It's good to be able to do the same thing in a number of different ways – this will stop your writing from becoming boring. The sentence looks smoother without big brackets cluttering it up.

Sense

This is really, really important. If you know how to section off words with commas, you will avoid some of the most **stupid** things that people do with punctuation.

Curse of the Killer Commas

They're out, of control.
And nothing, will ever, be quite, clear, again.
Appearing, now all over writing, everywhere.

Sometimes you must separate a word or a group of words from the rest of the sentence. Other times, you **must not.** Clearly, you need to know which one you're dealing with.

Look at this first example:

When I broke my leg a doctor was, happily, passing by.

This is fine. The main point of the sentence is that a doctor just happened to be walking past when I broke my leg. The word "happily" is an extra comment – telling us that the doctor passing by was a good thing. Because it's an extra comment, it's packaged off with the commas. So far, so good.

Now, just think how different the sense is if the commas are not there.

When I broke my leg a doctor was happily passing by.

Because the word "happily" hasn't been packaged off, it seems to be part of the main action. It makes it sound as if the doctor was passing by in a happy way. Of course, that might have been what happened, but if it's not what you meant to say, don't say it.

When I broke my leg a doctor was, happily, passing by.

When I broke my leg a doctor was happily passing by.

40

> I'll just, separate, everything, off, then.

No, Steven! Sometimes separating the words out makes you look very **stupid** indeed. Here's the rule:

When the words are needed for the sentence to make sense, and are **not** just an extra point, they should not be separated from the rest of the sentence.

Are the following right or wrong?

Questions

a) Ping-pong balls, made of steel, are not used in ping-pong tournaments.

b) Fish, living in water, are unaffected by air pollution.

c) Chinese men, who are over two metres tall, are few and far between.

Answers

✗ a) Wrong! By putting the words "made of steel" in between commas, they are made to look like extra information not needed for the sense. In other words, it looks as if the main part of the sentence is that ping-pong balls are not used in ping-pong tournaments, and by the way they are made of steel.

✔ b) Correct! All fish live in water, so you don't need the words "living in water". They are only there for emphasis, and so they can be packaged off with commas.

✗ c) Wrong! I hope you got this one. Again, by packaging off the words with the commas, it looks as if we have two pieces of information. One is that Chinese men are few and far between, and the other is that Chinese men are over two metres tall. Drop the commas and you'll see it makes sense.

Please place all watches, rings, jewellery, silly hats, money and valuables in the hotel safe.

If you want to write a list of things, the comma makes it easy to show which words are items on the list, and where the sense of the sentence starts again.

For safety reasons please do not take toys, rubber rings, submarines and pets into the pool.

Brenda Fishface
Lifeguard

You can see how helpful and important this is if you're listing groups of words, not just single words. Exactly the same rule applies:

For safety reasons please do not take silly toys, rubber rings of any description, submarines over 10 metres in length and dirty pets into the pool.

Doug E. Paddle

Imagine that without the commas. Nightmare.

It doesn't, of course, have to be a list of objects. You can have a list of events:

She came home, fed some vegetables, cooked the dog, went for a walk on the television, then watched the field for an hour before going to bath. It was time for some new glasses.

or instructions, like this:

I should go and have a break before you start the next section. You will need one teabag, a mug, a little milk, boiling water, and a clear head. Place the teabag in the mug, add the boiling water, remove the teabag, and add the milk. Pour the mixture slowly into your head.

Before you can have a go at sorting out some commas we'd better take a look at the Oxford comma.

You could say,"hammers, knives, guns and facemasks". But you could also say, "hammers, knives, guns, and facemasks". The extra comma before "and" in the second example is called the "Oxford comma". It's not wrong to use it but not many people do any more. Most people think that the "and" between the last things in the list gives enough of a pause by itself.

Where do you think the commas should be in these sentences?

Question 1

Steven forgot to put back into the car the engine the steering wheel the seats and the radio. The owner was surprised disappointed and upset when she came to collect it.

[No comma because it is still one item and hasn't changed into a list yet.]

[beginning of the list]

[list]

Answer 1

Steven forgot to put back into the car the engine, the steering wheel, the seats and the radio. The owner was surprised, disappointed and upset when she came to collect it.

[no need for Oxford comma]

[again no Oxford comma]

Question 2

The shop sold packs of dice cards marbles knives and Simon Cowell dolls.

Answer 2

The shop sold packs of dice, cards, marbles, knives, and Simon Cowell dolls.

Whether you need a comma after "knives" depends on what you are trying to say. If there is no comma, it would seem that there is one pack which includes knives **and** Simon Cowell dolls. This might be a fun pack to have. However, if you mean that there are separate packs for, on the one hand, knives, and, on the other, Simon Cowell dolls, you should put the extra comma in after "knives".

An adjective is a word that describes what a thing is like. For example, "green", "tall", "boring" and "beautiful" are all adjectives.

> What about lists of adjectives?

The tricky thing is that when you list a number of adjectives that apply to something, sometimes you put in commas and sometimes you don't. For example, some people write:

The long red velvet dress.

and some people write:

The long, red, velvet dress.

Don't worry that this isn't easy. On many occasions doing it either way will be right. But you do have to think about it because there are some times when getting it wrong would look pretty **stupid.** As in:

> He was a pretty violent man when confused by commas.

The word "pretty" is used here to mean "fairly" and goes with the "violent" to give a picture of someone who for some reason would get violent when faced with commas he couldn't handle. If you put a comma in the wrong place and said:

> He was a pretty, violent man when confused by commas.

it gets a bit strange. For some reason his confusion turns him "pretty" as well as "violent".

Where would you put the commas in these sentences?

Question 1

He looked at the knobbly green wax model of his face and thought how beautiful he was.

Answer 1

He looked at the knobbly green wax model of his face and thought how beautiful he was.
This is fine, but so is "knobbly, green, wax model".

Question 2

The castle was ancient famous airy and close to all local shops.

Answer 2

The castle was ancient, famous, airy and close to all local shops.
We need commas here because it's a list of features.

Question 3

The judge dealt with the matter fairly badly and quickly.

Answer 3

The judge dealt with the matter fairly badly and quickly.
If you put "fairly, badly and quickly' BAAAA! Wr-ong! That would mean that you should read "fairly" and "badly" as two different ways in which the judge dealt with it. But "fairly badly" should be read together – so don't separate the words with a comma.

USING COMMAS TO SET APART THE PEOPLE BEING ADDRESSED FROM THE REST OF THE SENTENCE

It seemed like a good idea at the time, officer.

Here a comma is used to tell you which bit of the sentence is there only to show who is being addressed. So, for example:

The commas show us that the words "ladies and gentlemen" are separate from the rest of the sentence. This makes it easier

> Someone, ladies and gentlemen, has been making allegations and I want to know who the alligator is.

to understand – just imagine it without the commas. It wouldn't be clear what was going on until you'd got a fair way into the sentence. In the same way:

> Are you going to meet Jeff, George?

Again, the comma makes it clear that the name at the end is set apart from the rest of the sentence. By having a comma, we know that there are two people in this sentence – Jeff and George. Without a comma, there would only be one – Jeff George. Once again, in a simple sentence, the meaning can be completely changed by missing out that tiny little comma.

See if you can work out what's happened on the next page.

IDIOT'S MISSING COMMA

Just another day in the office for private eye, Henry Bernstein.

From: Ian Idiot
To: Henry Bernstein

I want you to meet Lenny Henry. He may have some information on the stolen painting.

Bernstein tracks down Lenny Henry to New York.

This has cost a fortune. I hope Lenny Henry has some good information.

WALK

WALK FASTER

Hours later.

I'm terribly sorry, Mr Bernstein, I don't know what you are talking about. Ha ha ha.

Meanwhile back in London.

I wonder what's keeping Bernstein?

LENNY

STOLEN

MR IDIOT

Answer: Mr Idiot's mistake was to write "I want you to meet Lenny Henry" instead of "I want you to meet Lenny, Henry." It's his fault and it's going to cost him a lot of money.

USING COMMAS TO INTRODUCE DIRECT SPEECH
He dived across the beach shouting, "Mine! "Mine!

We'll come back to quoting people later. Just remember for the moment that you can introduce a quotation with a comma.

USING COMMAS TO INTRODUCE QUESTIONS
You are going to give me this video back, aren't you?

One way of asking a question is to make a statement, then add some words which turn it into a question, like "aren't you?" or "won't it?" or "isn't he?" That's nice and straightforward, isn't it?

The person speaking could have said:

But, by adding the extra bit he has made it clear what answer he expects – he really wants his video back.

> Are you going to give me my video back?

USING COMMAS TO EMPHASISE
I started fighting because I felt like it, that's why.

Just like our last example, a comma and an extra bit emphasises what has been said in the rest of the sentence.

USING COMMAS TO BALANCE TWO THINGS THAT ARE BEING COMPARED

The taller they are, the further they have to reach for their shoelaces.

If you imagine that each part of the sentence needs to be balanced, you can see how a comma separates off comparisons.

That's it for commas! Here's a short story to try out your comma skill. See in how many places there should be commas before looking at the answer. I've put in all the other bits of punctuation for you.

Question

It was a beautiful hot summer's day. The friends who had known each other for ten years had been playing all manner of games including rounders boules and volleyball. Although Terry Alderman had wanted to go home they were now playing cricket. He hit the ball high into the air. Joanna Mark Peggy and Sue all looked at each other. Mark spoke up.

"Well I can't catch that can I?" he said. "It's your turn Joanna."

Suddenly a bald man ran across the beach shouting "Duck!" The friends fell to the floor. To their surprise a large white duck flew over their heads with a wig in its beak.

[The information that Terry wanted to go home is separate from the friends playing cricket, so parcel off with a comma.]

[This is just an extra piece of information, so put commas in.]

Answer

It was a beautiful hot summer's day . The friends, who had known each other for ten years, had been playing all manner of games including rounders, boules and volleyball. Although Terry Alderman had wanted to go home, they were now playing cricket. He hit the ball high into the air. Joanna, Mark, Peggy and Sue all looked at each other. Mark spoke up.

[Comma not needed here, but it's a question of style – you might have put one in.]

[a list]

"Well, I can't catch that, can I?" he said. "It's your turn, Joanna."

[a question]

[comma separating out person addressed]

Suddenly a man ran across the beach shouting, [introducing direct speech]

[comma separating two pieces of information]

"Duck!" The friends fell to the floor. To their surprise, a large, white duck flew over their heads with a wig in its beak.

[adjective list]

49

I may be dull, but I think it's particularly important in a subject as difficult as this to summarise things clearly and in a neat way.

COLIN'S CONCLUSIONS PAGE

Commas show a slight pause in the sentence. Don't use a comma just because there is a pause – there may be a better way.

Commas:

set apart extra information (don't put information in commas if it is needed for the sentence to make sense)

separate items in a list

introduce direct speech

introduce questions

emphasise

balance comparisons

BRACKETS

Round Ones Looks Like This: ()

You can use brackets to add in an extra comment or fact to a sentence. For example:

Captain Finstaad (who had not seen a shop outside Norway before) was terribly impressed by the Mister Minit shoe-repair stand.

His son (who had travelled the world) was not.

If you took away the words in brackets, both sentences would still make perfect sense. But the information inside the brackets is actually very useful.

That's pretty much all there is to brackets, but you can use them in lots of different ways.

To explain something: The Duke's suicide note (which said, "The gun went off when I was cleaning it") was suspicious.

To add information: His dog (a pedigree poodle) wasn't much of a guard dog.

To add a comment: She was (hardly surprisingly) thrown out of the gang.

To add a reference: Her most telling admission (on page 68 of her book) was that she did goldfish impersonations.

To give examples and paint a picture: That afternoon, his mad activities (including an attempt to bite his own nose) attracted the attention of the mad police.

There are also square brackets which look like this: [ ]

These are not the same as ( ).

For a reason lost in the mists of time people call them "square brackets". Not really. I was just messing about. They're called square brackets because of their shape. They are usually put in by someone who did not write the rest of the sentence, in order to explain or add a comment on it. How about an example?

The person who is quoting this sentence wanted to explain who the "He" was. The square brackets make it clear that the words have been added later by someone else.

Mrs Scribble, the manageress of the high street bookshop, said "He [Tim de Jongh] is the author of some fantastic books".

Booknews

Mrs Scribble continued, "His books are much get better [sic] since there are more pictures in them."

Sometimes you might want to quote something and make it clear that you know it isn't written correctly. You can do this by putting the word "sic" into the passage in square brackets.

I accept (and this is a change from my previous view on this) that my clothes are way out of date. Perhaps I need a pair of trendy trainers to impress Zelda.

COLIN'S CONCLUSIONS PAGE

Brackets are useful for adding extra information into a sentence. This can be:

to give an explanation
to give information
to make a comment
to add a reference
to use examples to paint the picture.

COLONS

A Colon Looks Like This: :

That's given away the main use of a colon: to introduce something.

> Did you know that a large part of your stomach is called your "colon"?

If you find it helpful to think of the comma as something that says, "there will now be a short pause", think of the colon as saying: "Hey, look out everyone! Something's coming!"

These are the things a colon can introduce:

**lists
speech and quotations
questions
explanations.**

> Great! This is an excellent way to remember what it does. I can introduce the following things I like to eat with a colon: cake, chocolate, roast beef and curry.

Good grief! Let's look at that list of things a colon can introduce.

LISTS

This is the most common use of the colon. On the last page you read a list of things a colon can do, set out in "shopping list" form. But when writing sentences it's more usual to set out a list in the following way:

For the lovely "garlic brick" recipe on page 32, you will need the following: water, sand, grit, straw and garlic.

INTRODUCING SPEECH AND QUOTATIONS

We've already seen that you can introduce speech and quotations with a comma. You can also do it with a colon, if you like.

How about this:

Dr. Spock turned to Captain Kirk and said: "There's nothing wrong with him that a small head-removal operation wouldn't sort out."

If you read a play, you'll see the colon is used to introduce speech there, too. For example:

Steven: What did he just say?
Zelda: I think it was something about colons.
Steven: Oh! Shall we carry on now?

WARNING

Don't go colon crazy. Sometimes a sentence runs more smoothly without a colon before a list. For example, you shouldn't have a colon in this:

He was the school champion at: English, maths, history, and cheating.

It reads better and makes just as much sense if you do it without the colon, like this:

He was the school champion at English, maths, history, and cheating.

I bet you're asking, "What's the difference between this sentence and the one about the garlic brick?"

Look at the two sentences again.

In the "garlic brick" sentence we're told a list is coming. You can tell that there's almost a drawing in of breath before it starts. The list is a separate thing in itself. The colon says, "Hey, look there's something coming!"

In the "cheating" sentence, there's no real pause in the sense, is there? You could, if you wanted to, rewrite it like this:

He was the school champion in the following subjects: English, maths, history, and cheating.

But it doesn't flow when you read it like that, does it?

QUESTIONS

You can use a colon to introduce a direct question, like this:

> **The question addressed in Professor Bradshaw's article was simply this: does chocolate milk come from chocolate cows?**

EXPLANATION

You can also use a colon to introduce an explanation, like this:

> **Professor Bradshaw concluded that chocolate milk couldn't come from chocolate cows for one simple reason: the cows would melt in the summer.**

Important to remember

1. Don't use capitals after a colon unless the word that follows would have had a capital anyway.

2. Look at the list for the "garlic brick". The first word – "water" – doesn't have a capital. You use a capital only if the word following the colon would have had a capital letter anyway. For example. The football team had three great players: Roy of the Rovers, Mr Shaw and the Queen of England.

On the outside it's the Queen. She passes to Roy of the Rovers...

OK. Anyone who thinks they're a smartypants should try this. Where would you use a colon and where would you use a comma in the following?

I think that we're ready to try to spot two things at once.

Oh no we're not!

Question 1

If there were two things she hated more than being late, they were the following spinach stuck between her teeth without knowing about it and Simon Cowell coming to stay.

[introducing the next two things]

Answer 1

If there were two things she hated more than being late they were the following: having spinach stuck between her teeth without knowing about it, and Simon Cowell coming to stay.

[Although you could get away without having a comma here, a bit of a pause after the long first item would probably be helpful.]

Question 2

Jackson gave himself away with three tiny errors there was no 7:30 train on a Saturday the uncle's name was not John and he had a badge saying, "I'm the one who stole the painting".

[introducing a list]

Answer 2

Jackson gave himself away with three tiny errors: there was no 7:30 train on a Saturday, the uncle's name was not John, and he had a badge saying, "I'm the one who stole the painting".

[separating the items in the list]

[separating the items in the list]

To impress a girl like Zelda you need to be the following: fashionable, funny and able to sum up things in a clear way.

COLIN'S CONCLUSIONS PAGE

A colon is used to introduce:

lists (do you need a colon or would a list of commas be better?)

quotations (again commas are also possible)

questions

explanations.

SEMI-COLONS

The Semi-Colon Looks Like This: ;

It is made up of a comma and a full stop. Just like them, it marks a pause in a sentence. It is a bigger pause than a comma and a smaller pause than a full stop.

Judging the length of the pause you want is not always easy. After a while you get a feel for it. But until then you can survive without it. So don't get too hung up about it. Still, it is quite fun to have this little mark at the ready. If you know when it can be used, you're less likely to look **stupid** by slipping it in where it shouldn't be.

So, when do you use one?

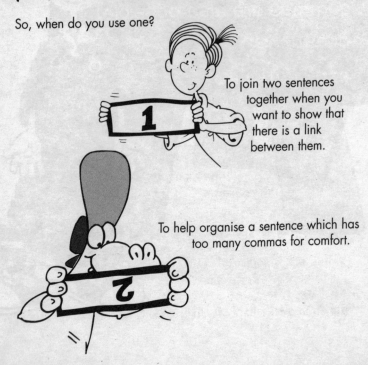

1 To join two sentences together when you want to show that there is a link between them.

2 To help organise a sentence which has too many commas for comfort.

60

Use a semi-colon instead of a joining word (like "and" or "but" or "because") between two sentences.

A He took the money. He was never seen again.

B He took the money and he was never seen again.

C He took the money; he was never seen again.

You can see that in **A** you can use two sentences, in **B** you can use "and" as a joining word, or if you are clever you could use **C** with a semi-colon.

Whhyyy do you need a semi-colon if you can use other ways to say it?

The Why Baby

By having less of a pause than a full stop, you bring the two sentences much closer together and you suggest that the two facts are linked. You could have used "and" but the semi-colon version is a bit punchier, isn't it? Think about that for these examples:

The woman kept coming back to the red car; you could tell she was interested.

The king looked over his subjects; he was quite tall.

This trick is particularly useful when you want to compare the two groups of words. For example:

Tim, who works hard, is rich; Jason, who doesn't, is happy.

WARNING

Use a semi-colon when you want to be dramatic. If you use it too much it will lose its impact and will look **STUPID.**

Also be careful that you use a semi-colon only to link sentences which are complete. If you want a pause in the middle of a sentence, you can either rewrite it or use a dash. For example:

✘ **He was a great actor; on most occasions.**

Wrong. The "on most occasions" isn't a full sentence. You still might want to have that dramatic pause before "on most occasions". But you can't do it with a semi-colon. So, try it with a dash:

✔ **He was a great actor — on most occasions.**

How can semi-colons help my comma confusion?

Sometimes you might want to write a sentence which, because it is complicated, needs a lot of pauses. For example:

The gang had four members: Zelda, a specialist in guns, explosives and welding equipment, Colin, the getaway driver, Steven, the strong man, and Bob Hoskins, who, in something of a mix-up, was on lead guitar.

There are far too many commas, aren't there? It looks ugly and I bet you got lost a couple of times.

You could rewrite it in shorter sentences, like this:

The gang had four members. There was Zelda, who was a specialist in guns, explosives and welding equipment. Colin was the getaway driver. Steven was the strong man. Bob...

Stop! Stop! DULL, DULL, DULL!

What we need is something to show which groups of words go together as one item in the list, and when we're moving on to the next person. The semi-colon comes to the rescue. Look:

Did somebody call?

The gang had four members: Zelda, a specialist in guns, explosives and welding equipment; Colin, the getaway driver; Steven, the strong man; and Bob Hoskins, who, in something of a mix-up, was on lead guitar.

Much easier. Do you see how the semi-colons separate the main groups of words in the list, and the commas are used within each group for more minor pauses?

Now you have a go at putting semi-colons and commas in this one.

Answer

The game "Snap" has not been made an Olympic sport for three reasons: it is too fast-moving, exciting and skilful for the television cameras; it is illegal in certain countries; and the President of the Olympic Federation lost his Aunt Edie, Uncle Bob, and his dog in a tragic card game accident.

Other people might say I have no chance with Zelda; I have yet to introduce her to my milk bottle top collection.

COLIN'S CONCLUSIONS PAGE

The semi-colon is a pause bigger than a comma, but smaller than a full stop.

Semi-colons join sentences together, linking sentences in a dramatic way.

They avoid comma confusion — use the commas to show minor pauses between the major pauses of the semi-colons.

DASHES AND DOTS

The Dash Looks Like This: —
Three Dots Look Like This: •••

First let's look at the dash. This is another punctuation mark which shows a pause in a sentence.

The dash can be used in lots of ways, for example —

Two dashes can be used — like this — as brackets.

A dash can be used to show that something is an afterthought — like this.

A dash can show — er — hesitation and — um — interruption.

A dash can introduce a list — of items, events, feelings or the uses of a dash.

A dash can just indicate a pause — for effect.

We'll go through these ways to use dashes — one by one.

BRACKETS

If you want to include some extra information, dashes work in the same way as brackets. Don't forget that it takes two dashes to parcel off the bit you want to separate.

If you would like an example – and I don't see why you shouldn't have one – then this will do.

Whhyyy use dashes if you could use brackets?

This is one of those style things again. But, if you compare these two sentences, you'll see that dashes give a slightly different effect than using brackets:

He was (thank heavens!) not a Spurs supporter.
He was – thank heavens! – not a Spurs supporter.

Don't you think that the dashes make the "thank heavens!" slightly more involved in the sentence?

AFTERTHOUGHTS

This is probably pretty obvious to you – or anyone else, for that matter.

HESITATION AND INTERRUPTION

Here the dash is particularly helpful if you're writing speech and you want to show that the speakers are being cut off in mid-sentence. Like this:

"I don't know how to say this –"
"What? Are you –"
"Please – let me – in my own way –"
"No! – I'm not listening –"

LISTS

In a list, the dash can be used in the same way as a colon. For example:

The first witch took out the materials — toe of frog, eye of bat, nose of stoat, finger of Britney Spears, and tongue of spam. The second witch decided she would dial out for a pizza instead.

PAUSES

Like a semi-colon, the dash can join two things together. For example:

"I never thought it was possible to die laughing — until you asked me to marry you," said Zelda to Colin.

But, unlike the semi-colon, the dash doesn't need those two things to be whole sentences. "Until you asked me to marry you" is not a full sentence, but with a dash you can use it anyway.

WARNING

Some people do not like the dash.

Why not—
it's nothing
to them,
surely?

Well, the dash can stand in for a number of other types of punctuation marks, but – and it's a big but – this is one reason it is not popular with some people. Because it can be used so easily, some **stupid** people use it all the time – to try to cover up the fact that they are not sure which other mark to use.

But look at that last paragraph. You can imagine that if you start using the dash too often, your writing might start to look a bit scrappy – breathless – out of control.

So, use it with care, or look  **STUPID.**

CONTINUING A WORD ON ANOTHER LINE

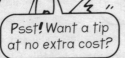

When you run out of space on your page and you can't fit in a long word, fortunately you can use a "-" to finish the word on the next line. Like I just have.

Psst! Want a tip at no extra cost?

Wait a minute, this wasn't mentioned as one of the things a dash does.

Ah, yes, well, there's a reason for that. As you know, this is a dash: –
This is a hyphen: -

Look similar, don't they?

The difference is that when the "-" occurs half way through a word, we call it a hyphen.

This speaks for itself, but there is one little thing you should know. If you do want to carry on a word on the next line, don't put the dash half-way through one of the syllables (the sounds that make up a word). Put it in the space between the sounds.

For example, don't say that Steven is stupi-
d.

If you really can't fit it on one line, say that he is stupid.

Thank you.

Now let's look at the three dots.

You remember that they look like this:... They are sometimes called a "three dot ellipsis". They show that something has been missed out.

You can use them if you want to use parts of a long quotation but leave other bits out. So, instead of:

Wing Commander Fanbelly wrote, "Of all the many examples of stupid behaviour by the R.A.F., and let me say I am ashamed to admit there has been a very large number of such examples in my short time with the service, I think that trying to fly without wings or any form of power was the stupidest."

You could just put:

Wing Commander Fanbelly wrote, "Of all the many examples of stupid behaviour by the R.A.F.,... trying to fly without wings or any form of power was the stupidest".

This makes it plain to the reader that you have quoted just some of the words he used.

Sometimes, the three dots are used to show that something is left out, with the reader being expected to know what it is. For example:

The R.A.F. has done some stupid things in its time, but trying to fly without wings or any form of power...

Here the writer is saying, "You don't need me to finish this sentence for you, do you?" Or it can be that the three dots just show the passing of time, for example:

"Darling, I don't know how to say this."
He felt a bang on his head, then everything went black...
When he woke up, he was surrounded by people looking at him and making fun of his hair.

Some more examples...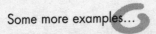

Hold on! This is wrong! Whoever wrote this is **stupid** because thay are trying to show that something is coming up. But as we know, that's the function of the colon or the dash.

Here are some more examples:

Question

Which of the following is wrong?

a   She walked back to the door (if at first you don't succeed...), but then something made her stop.

b   It was just that I thought I might... No, don't bother.

c   The more Peter threw yoghurt at her... the more irritated she became.

Answer

c is wrong, because:

a   The three dots stand for the rest of the saying (try, try, again).

b   The speaker tails off and the rest of the sentence is left unfinished – missed out.

c   Nothing has been missed out here. OK, so you want a pause, but a comma would do just fine.

I think — I'm not sure — Zelda may be washing her hair on the evening I would like to show her my milk bottle tops.

COLIN'S CONCLUSIONS PAGE

Dashes can be used for —
    brackets
    afterthoughts
    introducing a list
    a pause for effect.
        Don't overuse them.

Three dots can be used to:
    show something is missed out
    (eg. in quotations)
    ask the reader to fill in the gap.

Don't use them to introduce things.

APOSTROPHES

An Apostrophe Looks Like This: '

So, does a catastrophe look like this?

Ha, ha, very funny. Now, pay attention.

What you have to remember is that the apostrophe has two very common, but very different, uses.

It can show **possession.** This means that one thing **belongs** to another. For example: Steven's warts. This means that the warts belong to Steven. Lucky Steven!

It can show **omission.** This means that something has been **missed** out. For example, you might write, "Steven's stupid". Written out in full, this would be "Steven is stupid". The apostrophe is to show that the "i" of "is" has been missed out – omitted.

Now, we'll have a look at how each of them works, but first remember this:

Every time you're about to write an apostrophe:

THINK.
Do I want to show possession or omission?
If I don't, I should not be using an apostrophe.

When you have decided that you are showing possession or omission:

THINK.
Where should I put the apostrophe?

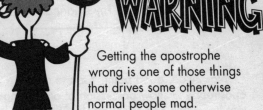

WARNING

Getting the apostrophe wrong is one of those things that drives some otherwise normal people mad.

Possession

To show ownership, normally you just add an apostrophe and "s" to the thing that is doing the owning, and then write the thing owned. So:

"The spanner of Zelda" becomes "Zelda's spanner".

"The warts of Steven" becomes "Steven's warts".

I'm upset by the "warts". I mean I'm quite fond of them, but shouldn't they have an apostrophe like this: wart's?

Read the first sentence of this section again, Steven. You only add the apostrophe to the thing doing the owning, not the thing owned. The word "warts" has an "s" because there is more than one wart, not because the warts own anything. So no apostrophe.

This isn't just about owning objects, like my spanner, is it?

No, Zelda, good point. You use an apostrophe to show possession of other things too. You could say, for example, "Stephen's lack of understanding was complete".

How would you rewrite the following sentences using the apostrophe?

a The friends of Alison.
b The visiting hours of the local witch-doctor.
c The hairs on my chinny-chin-chin.
d The rules of the apostrophe are less difficult than some people think.
e It was the habit Sheila had of dancing round her handgun that Bruce found so surprising.
f The late goal scored by Arsenal caused the relegation of Norwich City.

Answers

a Alison's friends.
b The local witch-doctor's visiting hours.
c My chinny-chin-chin's hairs.
d The apostrophe's rules are less difficult than some people think.
e It was Sheila's habit of dancing round her handgun that Bruce found so surprising.
f Arsenal's late goal caused Norwich City's relegation.

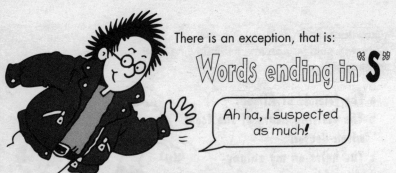

There is an exception, that is:

Words ending in "S"

Ah ha, I suspected as much!

If the word doing the owning already ends in "s", you have to be a little more careful. There are two rules. What you do depends on whether the word is **singular** (just the one thing, eg. James) or **plural** (more than one thing, eg. boys).

If the owning word is plural, eg. boys, you don't need to add another one. Just add an apostrophe after the "s" that is already there. So:

1

"The bravery of the soldiers" becomes "The soldiers' bravery".
"The hats of the girls" becomes "The girls' hats".

Lots of people get confused and think that the word must have a "s" at the end, or they move the apostrophe, or drop it, or panic and put it everywhere, as in **"The boys' tenni's ball's"** which just looks silly.

Keep calm. Always think about the word doing the owning; in this case, "boy". Before you start adding the apostrophe, is there one or more boy? For example, if you want to say that one boy had some tennis balls, you would write:

The boy's tennis balls.

Because the word doing the owning here doesn't end in "s", it's the normal rule. If you had three boys with tennis balls you would write:

The boys' tennis balls.

I see. So if I discovered that all my warts have hairs, instead of saying "The hairs of my warts", I could say, "My warts' hairs".

Yes, I'm afraid you could, Steven. Oh, dear, how disgusting! What a shame you're still here!

But if I only had one wart, it would be "My wart's hairs".

Shut up, Steven. Shut up. SHUT UP. But you are right, for a change.

If the word is **singular** and ends in "s", eg. James, you add an apostrophe and "s" as normal.

For example: if you wanted to say, "The bicycle of James", you could say "James's bicycle".

If you wanted to say "The neighbours of the Jones family" you could say "The Jones's neighbours".

Ready for the next stage?

Now, one strange thing that you just have to remember. You just have to remember **it**.

It

The word "it" is an exception to the normal rule on possession.

Tell us about it.

Sometimes you'll want to say "of it", as in, "The smell of it was awful". If you followed the normal rule of adding an apostrophe and "s" to "it" (the thing doing the owning), you would get:

It's smell was awful.

Don't

Instead, you say "its", without the apostrophe. So:

Its smell was awful.

There is a good reason for this. In the word "it's", the apostrophe only ever shows that something is missing (we'll be looking at this next), so in "It's been lovely to see you", the "It's" is short for "It has". And in "It's a lovely day", the "It's" is short for "It is".

Before we leave this, Zelda, my glamorous assistant, will hold up some important words. These words do not have apostrophes even though they do show possession.

Yours, his, hers, ours, theirs, whose

Now your turn. Where would you put apostrophes in this lot?

[This is short for "It is",
so you use the apostrophe.]

[It is the father of Edward, so add and
apostrophe and "s" to Edward.]

Answer
"Whose football is this?" asked Edward's father.
"It's Bill's said Edward.

[This is short for "It is the football of Bill" so it's Bill's football.]

"And what is the colour of this football?" thundered Edward's
mad Uncle Arthur.

[same as for Edward's father]

[No apostrophe here
as this means "of it".] "Its colour is blue," said Edward.

[exception word]

"Speak up, lad!" shouted Arthur, whose hearing was not good.

[This is short
for "It is".] "It's blue," repeated Edward.
"And whose lawn is this?" the adults'

[The word "adults"
ends in "s".]

voices chimed in together.

[short
for "it is"] "It's the Jones's [meaning belonging to the Jones family].
They have been its [Here it means possession.] owners since
1872," persisted Edward.

Omission

Now for something easier.

An apostrophe can also be used to show that something has been left out – omitted. Usually it's when two words have been run together.

Look at the "it's" in the last sentence. It is actually "it is" run together. The apostrophe shows that the "i" in "is" has been dropped.

So when I say "This car's not going to start", the apostrophe in "car's" shows that it's short for "car is", but the "i" is missing.

Quite, and you've put the apostrophe in "it's" correctly as well. Well done.

Here are some more examples:

you will = you'll
that is = that's
can not = can't
you are = you're
does not = doesn't
is not = isn't
of the clock = o'clock

we are = we're
he had = he'd
all is = all's
he will not = he won't
it is = it's

Flashback

Finally, a quick reminder about the apostrophe and "it". You only use "it's" when you mean "it is" or "it has". When you want to show that something belongs to "it" you say "its".

There are lots of examples of this. Can you think of any, Steven?

I've gone blank, sorry. Let's see. I'll try, but I'm not sure it'll come to me in time — it's quite hard.

Six! Very well done!

What?

Oh, never mind.

Hold on before you turn the page. Why do we say "he won't" for "he will not"?

Well spotted — just testing. It looks like a strange exception, but actually it's because "wol" was the old way of saying "will". You don't have to remember that, but you do have to put "won't" and not "willn't".

Can you see what is right and what is wrong with this sentence?

Answer

Computers, which are made of jelly, have proved it's true that you'll live to be 168 without breathing if you wear a hat made from a sailor's ration of peas, despite its unpleasant smell.

"Computer's" is wrong because it's just the plural of computer. It's nothing to do with ownership and there's no letter missed out. Also, "you'll" is short for "you will" and so needs an apostrophe. There should be an apostrophe in "sailor's" to show that the ration belongs to a sailor. (If it belonged to lots of sailors it would be "sailors'.") There shouldn't be one in "peas" because it's just a plural. Finally, "its" shouldn't have an apostrophe here as it doesn't mean "it is" or "it has".

Now you know how it works, sit back and have a laugh about how **stupid** this person looked when he just put one tiny apostrophe in the wrong place in this letter.

Dear Cheryl,
My beloved. I have just left Morocco forever. The customs officer forced me to leave my pet dog's behind. It was such a sad moment. It reminded me of the time I had to leave you — and your sad face on the other side of the barrier.
Write soon.
Gerhardt.

I've told Zelda that we're going to see a great film about the history of gravel. Its title is "Dull Days Outdoors".

COLIN'S CONCLUSIONS PAGE

The apostrophe shows:
Possession
Add "s" to the owning word, then put the thing owned, eg. the boy's books.

If the owning word already has an "s":

If it's plural, put the " ' " after the "s" that's already there, eg. the boys' books.

If it's singular, add " 's " as normal eg. James's book.

Remember: an apostrophe shows that something is missing, eg. it's, they'll, we'll, o'clock.

QUOTATION MARKS

Quotation Marks are also called Inverted Commas and Sometimes also Speech Marks
They Look Like This: ' ' (Single) or Like This: " " (Double)

There are two ways in which you can show what someone else has said. You can actually say the exact words that were said. (This is called **direct** speech.) So:

Well, I'm sorry but I would rather stick needles in my eyes than go out with Colin.

would be written as:

"Well, I'm sorry but I would rather stick needles in my eyes than go out with Colin," Zelda told me.

Or you can say what the person meant, by summarising what they said, without actually repeating it word for word. (This is called "indirect" speech – because we are not hearing directly the words that were spoken.) So:

Steven's Diary - Friday 13th
Zelda said ~~that she would rather stick needles in her eyes~~ ~~than go out with Colin. Zelda said she did not wish~~ ~~to go out with Colin.~~ Zelda apologised, saying that there were other activities which she felt were more appealing than going out with Colin.

As you can see, quotation marks tell us that the words set out between them were the exact words used. This can be useful to tell when we're reading exactly the words that were spoken, and when we have to bear in mind that they are being reported through someone else's choice of words.

How do I show quotes within quotes?

You can use a different pair of quotation marks for the second quote. So if you normally use double quotation marks, you use singles as the inside pair. For example:

He said, "I've seen *Shrek 2* four thousand times."

How do I make it clear who I'm quoting?

You should always make sure it's clear. For example:

The head zookeeper at London Zoo described lions as "the fluffiest little cats on earth".

Look how irritating it is when it is not clear who is speaking:

**Michael, Samantha and Barry went to the kitchen.
"I think it's time," said Samantha, "to sort out who the killer is."
"Who are you looking at?"
"Well, it was you standing over the body with a smoking gun in your hand saying, 'Right, that's her shot. Now I'll get the inheritance money', wasn't it?"
"OK, so it was me."
"I knew it."**

Now, whodunnit? I dunnoit.

WHAT EVERYONE GETS CONFUSED ABOUT

It's not so much the quotation marks that people get confused about, as what to do with all the other punctuation marks in the area. Do you put the full stop inside or outside the quotation marks? Where do you put commas? When do you have capital letters?

Don't worry! Here are the answers.

Introducing a Quotation

When you're introducing a quotation, use a comma to indicate the pause between the rest of the sentence and the quoted bit. For example:

He looked her straight in the eye and said, "You've got something in your eye."

Advanced Students Only

You are allowed to use a colon instead.

The quotation here is a complete sentence, and so the quoted bit begins with a capital letter, "Y".

Because it's a complete sentence, that's "Y".

You use the comma in the same way when you want to put the quotation first. Then the pause comes after the quote, for example:

"I'd like a fried potato slice," he said, crisply.

And here's another thing to remember when writing down speech.

space "You might have noticed that

each new speaker goes on a new line."

space "You might also have noticed

that each of these "new" lines is

indented."

Finally, you don't have to bother with the comma to introduce the quotation if you're not quoting a full sentence. For example:

> The dentist said my
> teeth were "yellowy and rubbish".

That's it for introducing quotations. The other things that are confusing are interrupting a quotation, and finishing one. We'll move onto them straightaway.

INTERRUPTING A QUOTATION

Sometimes you might want to interrupt a quotation. For example:

"I suppose it's possible," said Mr. Dull, "that the party will be fun without me. I rather doubt it."

Now, do you use a capital letter when you go back to the quotation after interrupting it?

The answer is: it depends on where you've interrupted the quotation.

If you've interrupted it between sentences, you restart with a capital letter.

If you've interrupted it mid-sentence, you carry on as normal with a small letter. So, the above example is correct, and so is:

"I suppose it's possible that the party will be fun without me," said Mr. Dull. "I rather doubt it."

ENDING A QUOTATION

We're now going to look at the bit that really sends people bonkers.

The good news is, it's not that hard. So, by reading the next page and putting in a bit of effort, you can not only avoid looking STUPID you can actually look clever instead.

The question is always: "Which bits go inside the quotation marks, and which bits go outside?"

The answer is: punctuation marks go inside the quotation marks if they are only to do with the words inside the quotation marks, but outside if they are part of the whole sentence.

Do you remember Mr. Dull's comments about the party? Look back at where the full stops were.

What about this example:

He hissed, "Don't do it!"

The exclamation mark is there to show that the words "Don't do it" are to be given more emphasis than normal. So, as the exclamation mark goes with the words "Don't do it", it goes inside the quotation marks.

If the words "Don't do it" had been said in a normal way, but it was a surprise that they had been said, the exclamation mark would be outside the quotation marks, like this:

To my amazement, he simply said, "Don't do it."!

For a question mark, the same rule applies. For example:

She asked him, "Will you marry me?"

The question is completely within the quotation marks – so the question mark goes within them, too. But how about this:

Did she ask him, "Will you marry me"?

Strictly speaking, this should be:

Did she ask him, "Will you marry me?"?

This is because both the quoted words and the whole sentence are questions.

When this happens, you should put the question mark outside the quotation marks only. So the longer question (that is the whole sentence) gets the question mark and not the smaller one.

I no longer need to say, I may be dull. From now on I will be able to impress with my punctuation.

COLIN'S CONCLUSIONS PAGE

Quotation marks show direct speech. Always make sure it's clear who's saying what. Quotes within quotes need a different type of quotation mark to the ones you usually use.

Introduce a quotation with a comma (or a colon) before a quote, or a comma within the quotation marks at the end.

If you interrupt a quotation, the word that follows the new quotation mark only has a capital letter if it's a new sentence or if you would use a capital letter for the first word anyway.

When you end a quotation, put the final bit of punctuation inside the quotation marks if it is to do with the words in the quotation, outside if it completes the whole sentence.

THE FINAL TEST

Now it's time to test you on everything. Get a pen and paper and see if you can write out the following passage, punctuating it correctly.

colin who was a good if dull man was thinking of what zelda might want to do they could have a nights clubbing see colins favourite film or go out for a meal suddenly colin had an idea zelda he said what would you say if i invited you to see my gravel collection thats easy said zelda id say no thank you colin its dull

Now check your answer and count up your mistakes.

Colin, who was a good (if dull) man, was thinking of what Zelda might want to do: they could have a night's clubbing; see Colin's favourite film; or go out for a meal.
Suddenly, Colin had an idea. "Zelda," he said, "what would you say if I invited you to see my gravel collection?"
"That's easy," said Zelda. "I'd say, "No thank you Colin, it's dull."

How well did you do?

25 mistakes or more
Well, there wasn't much point you doing it, was there Steven?

20-24 mistakes
Well, you haven't done that well, I'm afraid. Read the book again and you'll do better next time.

15-19 mistakes
Not disastrous at all, because there are a lot of tricky points here, but you should check the bits you got wrong and then have another go.

10-14 mistakes
Better than average - well done! But still not quite good enough. So have another go after looking up the things you got wrong.

5-9 mistakes
Great! Congratulations! You've passed! Turn the page and collect your certificate.

0-4 mistakes
You are either a cheat, or one of the finest punctuators in the country. If it's the latter, turn over and get your certificate now.

The M.O.P. Certificate
(Ministry of Punctuation)

This is to certify that ....

(hereinafter referred to as "the holder of this certificate") can punctuate.

This entitles the holder of this certificate to:

- greater confidence when writing

- more respect from any reader of the writing
of the holder of this certificate

- be a bit uppity with people who can't punctuate

- a fabulous life uninhindered by the nerves and shame
of an inability to punctuate.

Most of all, the holder of this certificate will never, ever look STUPID.

Note this all ye who read.

CONGRATULATIONS!